FINGERPICKING BALLADS

ISBN 978-0-634-09893-2

HAL•LEONARD®
CORPORATION
7777 W. BLUEMOUND RD. P.O. BOX 13819 MILWAUKEE, WI 53213

T0026085

Visit Hal Leonard Online at
www.halleonard.com

Against All Odds

(Take a Look at Me Now)

Words and Music by Phil Collins

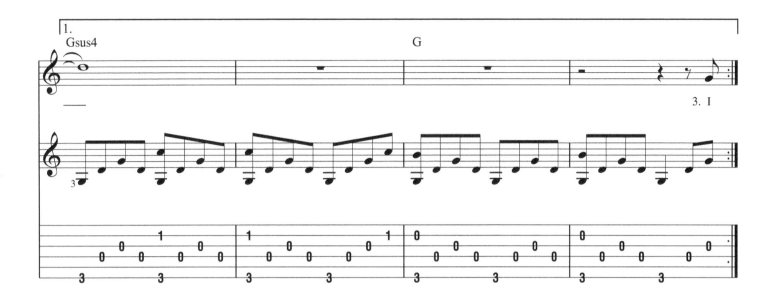

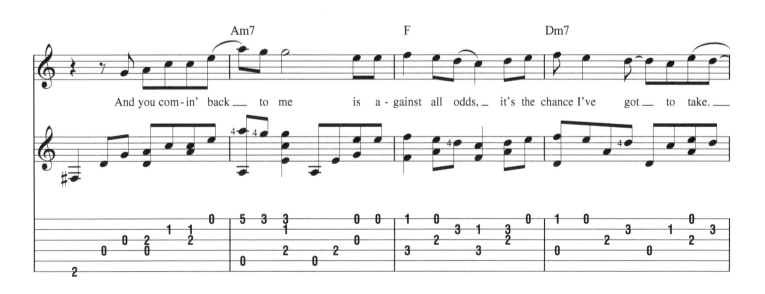

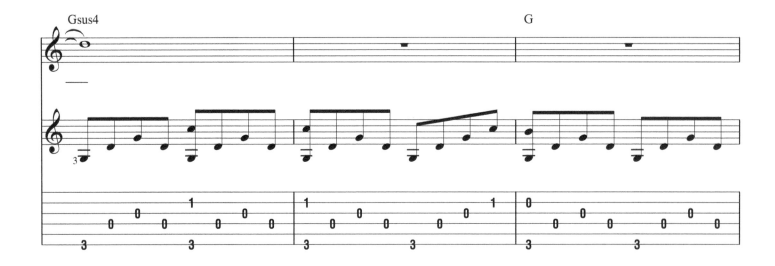

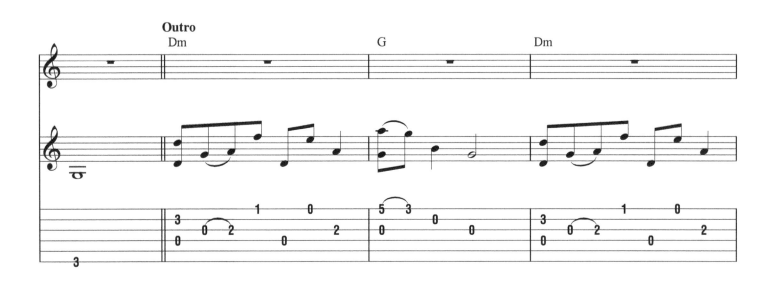

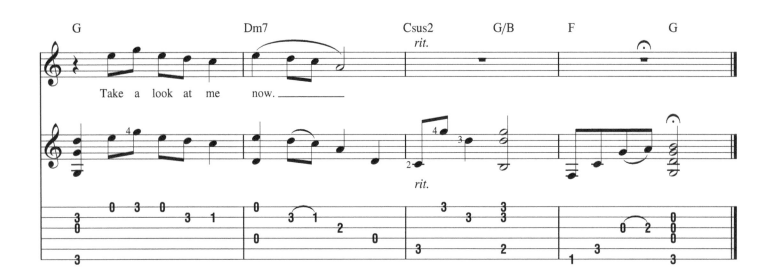

Take a look at me now. _____

Additional Lyrics

3. I wish I could just make you turn around,
   Turn around and see me cry.
   There's so much I need to say to you,
   So many reasons why.
   You're the only one who really knew me at all.

Have I Told You Lately

Words and Music by Van Morrison

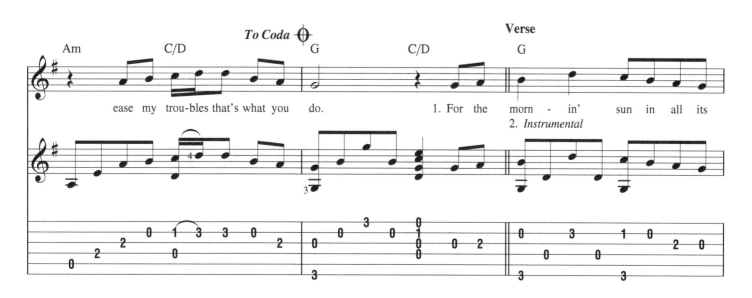

Alone

Words and Music by Billy Steinberg and Tom Kelly

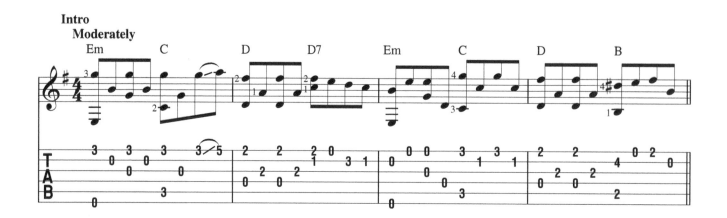

1. I hear the tick-ing of the clock.   I'm ly-ing here, the room's pitch dark.
2. *See additional lyrics*

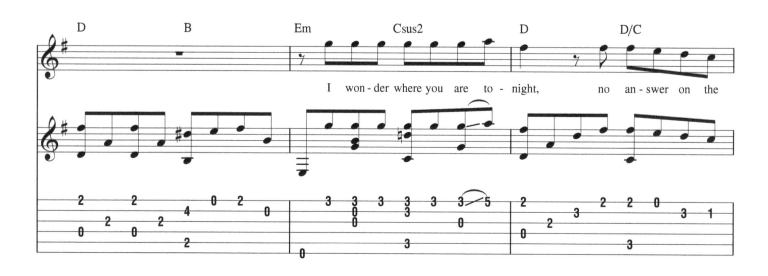

I won-der where you are to-night,   no an-swer on the

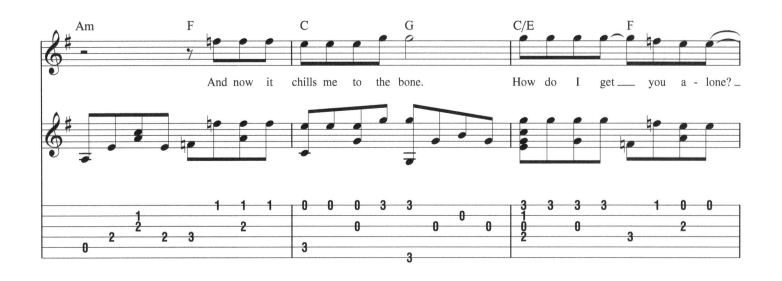

And now it chills me to the bone. How do I get___ you a - lone?___

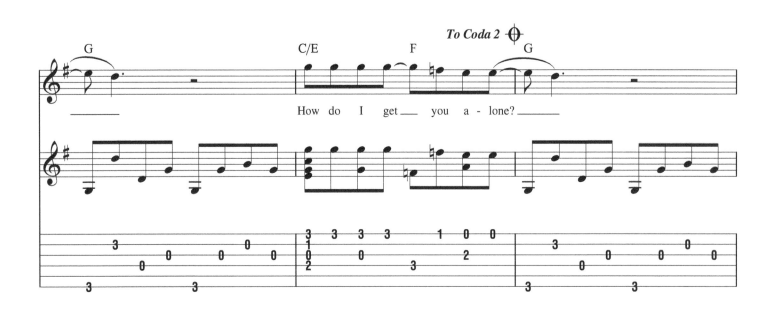

To Coda 2

How do I get___ you a - lone?_____

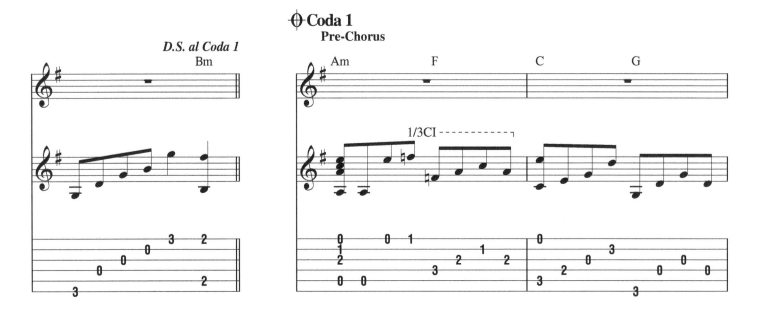

Coda 1
Pre-Chorus

D.S. al Coda 1

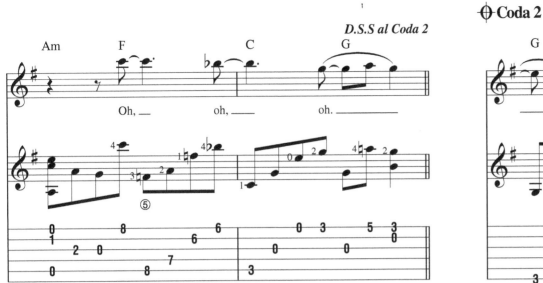

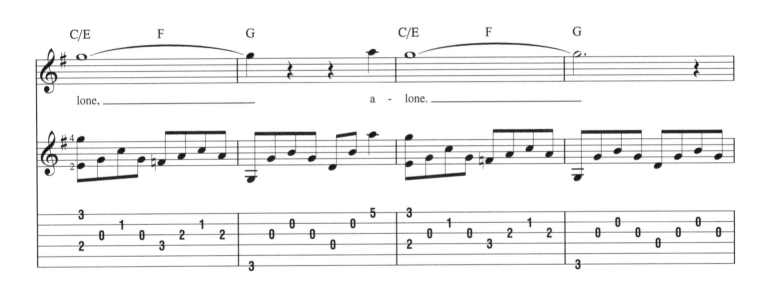

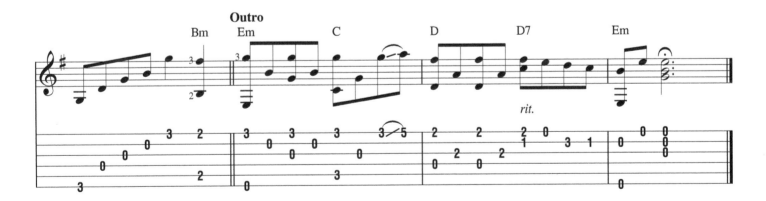

Additional Lyrics

2. You don't know how long I have wanted
To touch your lips and hold you tight, oh.
You don't know how long I have waited,
And I was gonna tell you tonight.
But the secret is still my own,
And my love for you is still unknown.
Alone.

(Everything I Do) I Do It for You

from the motion Picture ROBIN HOOD: PRINCE OF THIEVES

Words and Music by Bryan Adams, Robert John Lange and Michael Kamen

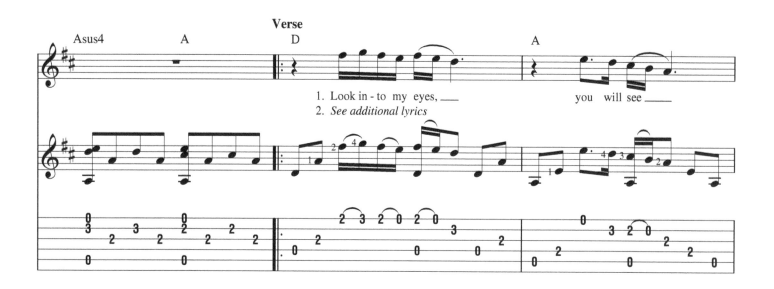

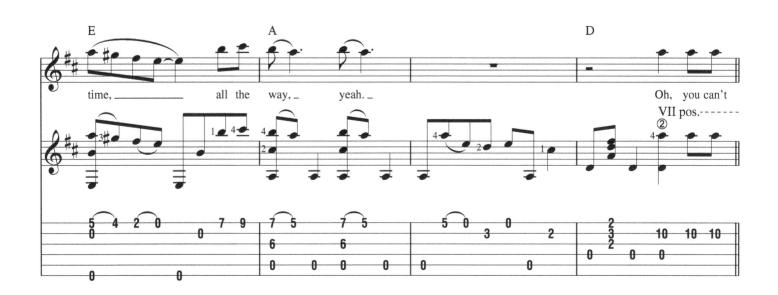

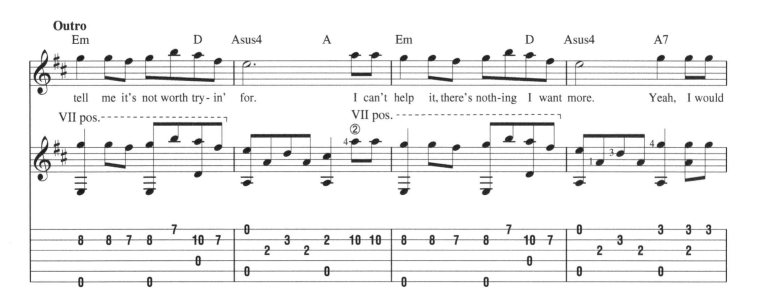

fight — for you, — I'd lie — for you, — walk the wire for you, — yeah, I'd

die for you. — You know it's true, ev-'ry-thing I

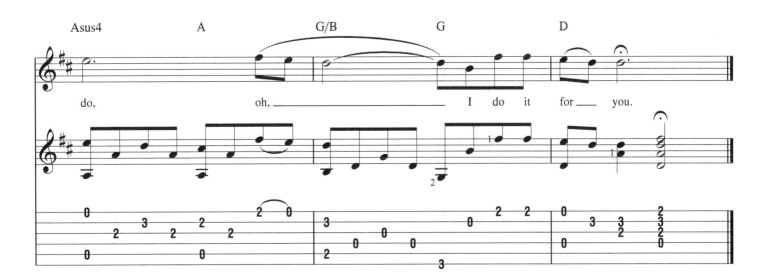

do, oh, — I do it for — you.

Additional Lyrics

2. Look into your heart, you will find,
   There's nothing there to hide.
   Take me as I am, take my life,
   I would give it all, I would sacrifice.
   Don't tell me it's not worth fighting for.
   I can't help it, there's nothing I want more.
   You know it's true, ev'rything I do,
   I do it for you.

Fields of Gold

Music and Lyrics by Sting

Verse

Moderately

1. You'll re - mem-ber me, __ when the west wind moves, __ up - on the fields __ of bar -
3. *See additional lyrics*

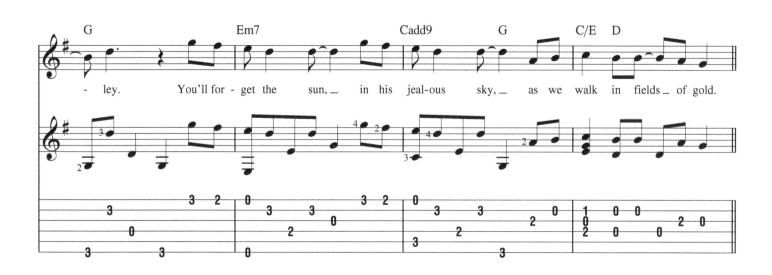

- ley. You'll for - get the sun, __ in his jeal-ous sky, __ as we walk in fields __ of gold.

Interlude

2. So she
4. *See additional lyrics*

took her love,_ for to gaze a - while,_ up - on the fields_ of bar - ley. In his

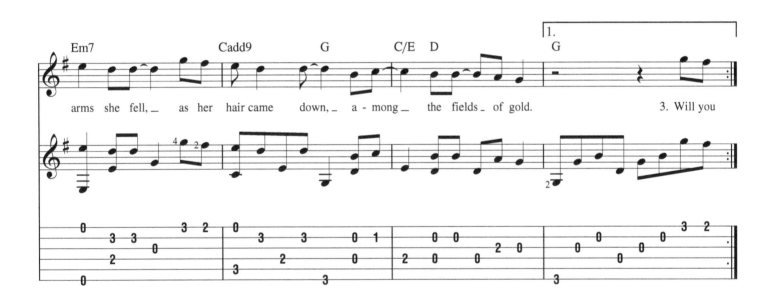

arms she fell,_ as her hair came down,_ a - mong_ the fields_ of gold. 3. Will you

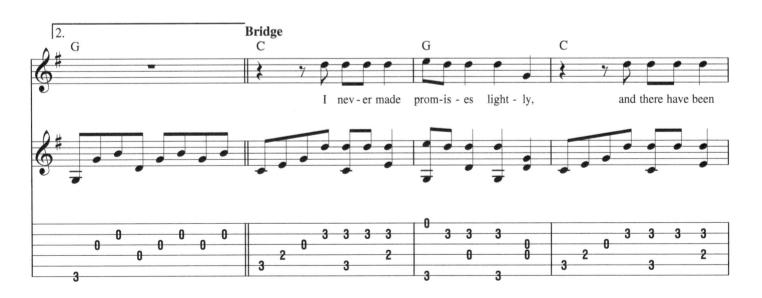

I nev - er made prom - is - es light - ly, and there have been

some that I've bro - ken. But I swear, _ in the days still left, we'll walk _ in fields _ of gold.

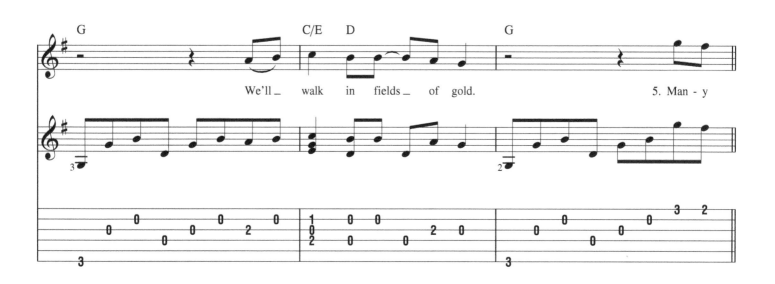

We'll _ walk in fields _ of gold. 5. Man - y

Verse

years have passed _ since those sum - mer days, _ a - mong the fields _ of bar - ley. See the

6. *See additional lyrics*

Additional Lyrics

3. Will you stay with me, will you be my love,
   Among the fields of barley?
   We'll forget the sun in his jealous sky,
   As we lie in fields of gold.

4. See the west wind move, like a lover so,
   Upon the fields of barley.
   Feel her body rise, when you kiss her mouth
   Among the fields of gold.

6. You'll remember me, when the west wind moves,
   Upon the fields of barley.
   You can tell the sun, in his jealous sky,
   When we walked in fields of gold,
   When we walked in fields of gold,
   When we walked in fields of gold.

From a Distance

Words and Music by Julie Gold

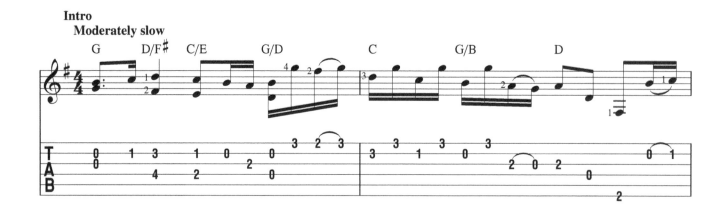

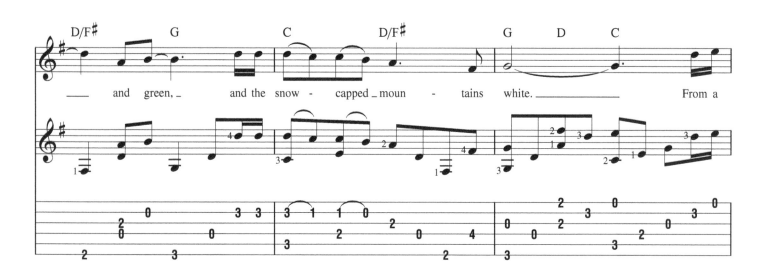

2. From a man. God _ is watch-ing us. _ God _ is

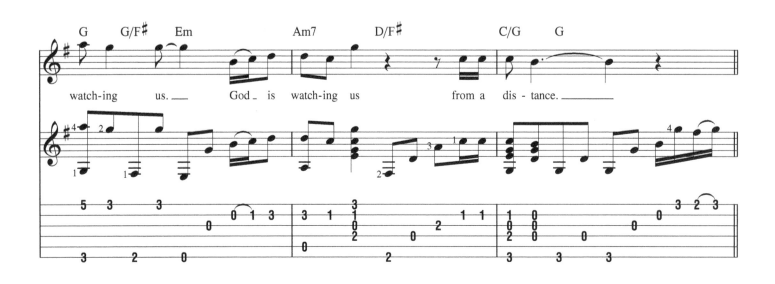

watch-ing us. _ God _ is watch-ing us from a dis - tance. _____

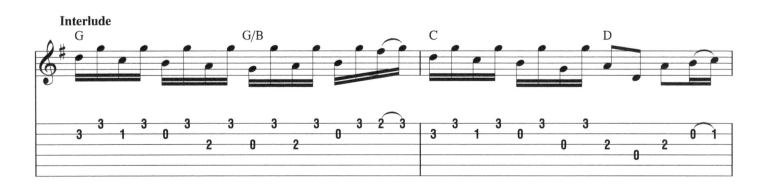

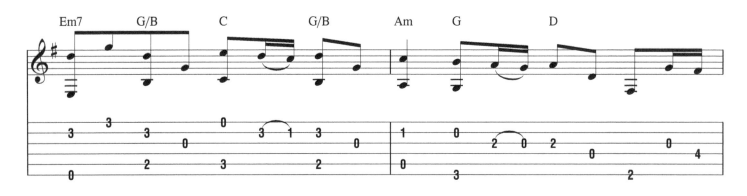

Additional Lyrics

2. From a distance we all have enough, and no one is in need.
And there are no guns, no bombs, and no disease, no hungry mouths to feed.
From a distance we are instruments marching in a common band
Playing songs of hope, playing songs of peace. They're the songs of every man.

3. From a distance you look like my friend, even though we are at war.
From a distance I just cannot comprehend what all this fighting is for.
From a distance there is harmony, and it echoes through the land.
And it's the hope of hopes, it's the love of loves. It's the heart of every man.

Hard to Say I'm Sorry

Words and Music by Peter Cetera and David Foster

Drop D tuning:
(low to high) D–A–D–G–B–E

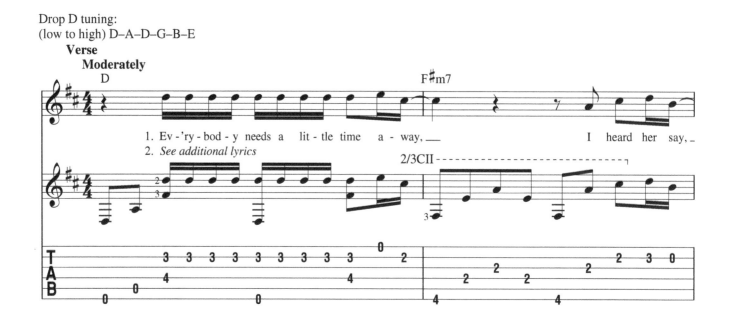

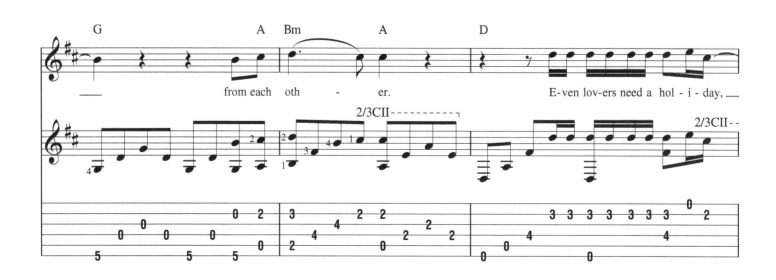

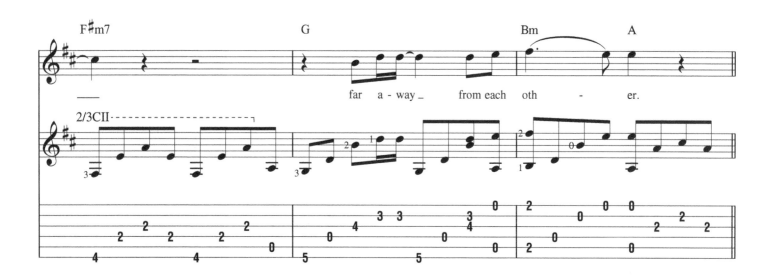

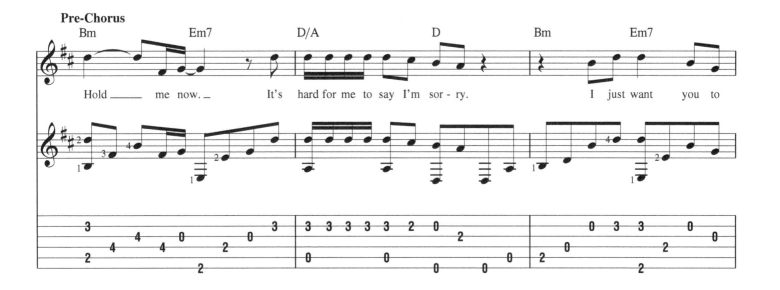

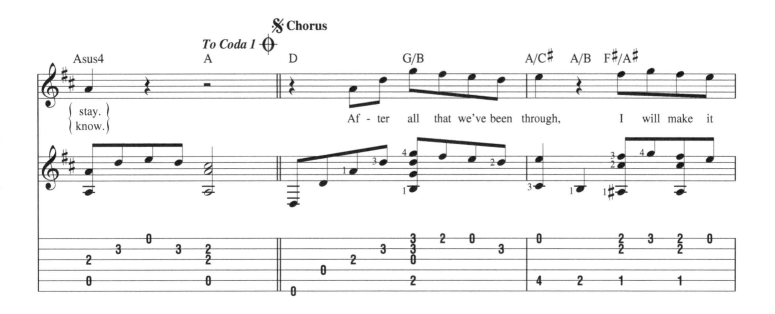

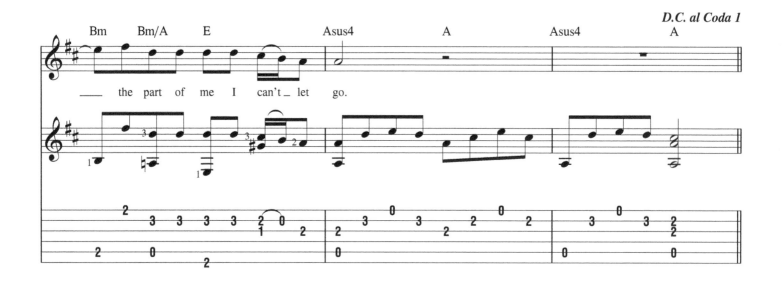

⊕ Coda 1

⊕ Coda 2

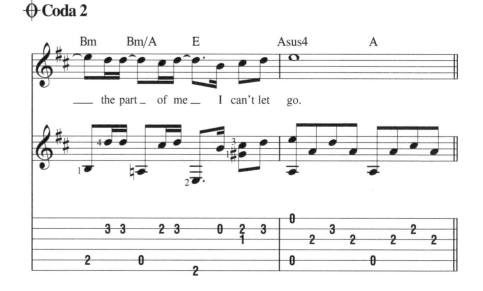

Outro-Chorus

Af - ter all that we've been through, I will make it up to you. I'll prom -

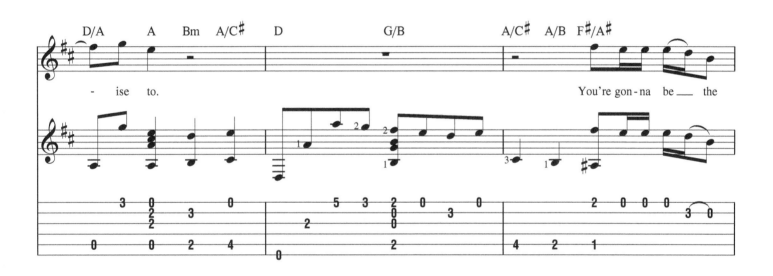

- ise to. You're gon - na be ___ the

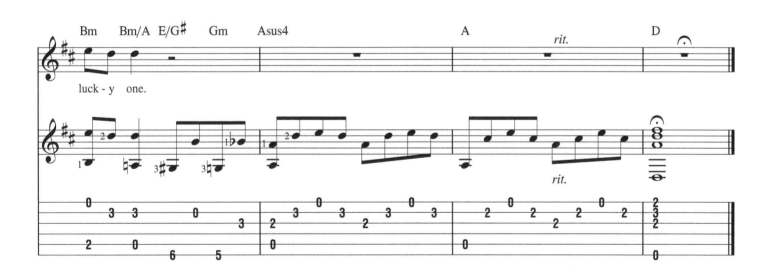

luck - y one.

Additional Lyrics

2. Couldn't stand to be kept away,
   Just for the day, from your body.
   Wouldn't wanna be swept away,
   Far away, from the one that I love.

I'll Be There for You

Words and Music by Jon Bon Jovi and Richie Sambora

Drop D tuning:
(low to high) D–A–D–G–B–E

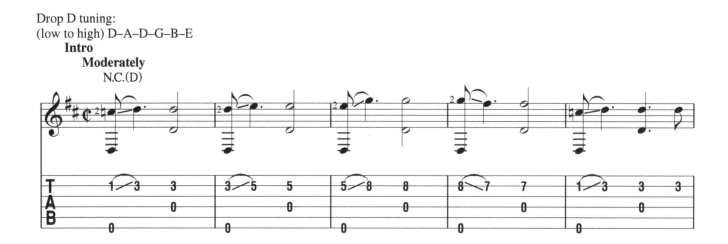

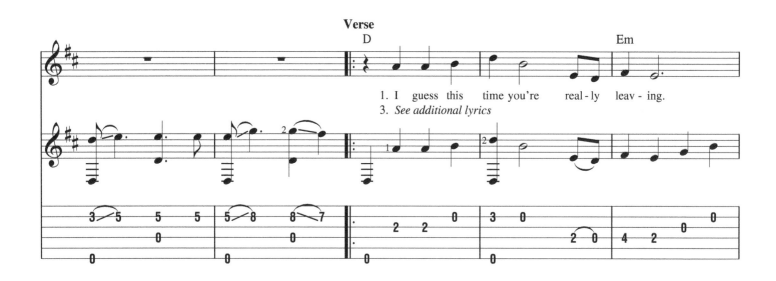

1. I guess this time you're real-ly leav-ing.
3. *See additional lyrics*

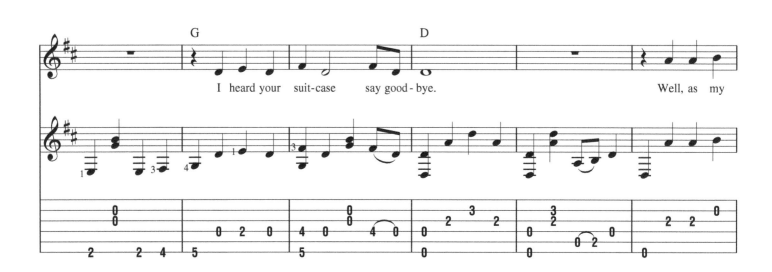

I heard your suit-case say good-bye.

Well, as my

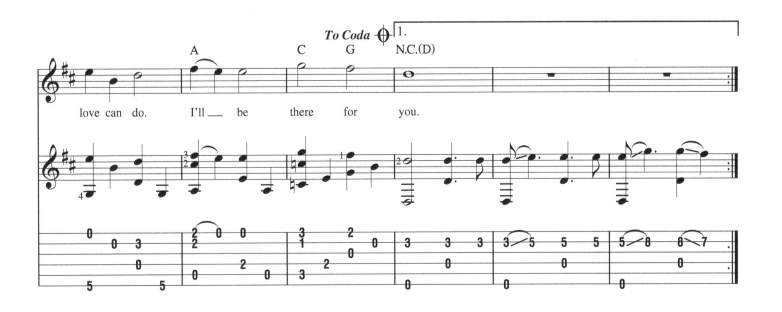

love can do. I'll ___ be there for you.

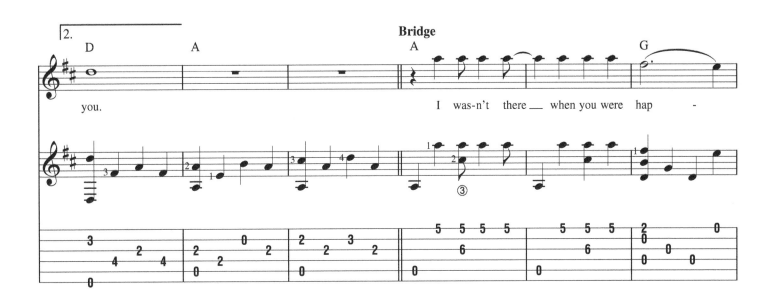

you.

Bridge

I was-n't there ___ when you were hap -

py, and I was-n't there ___ when you were down, _____ child. _

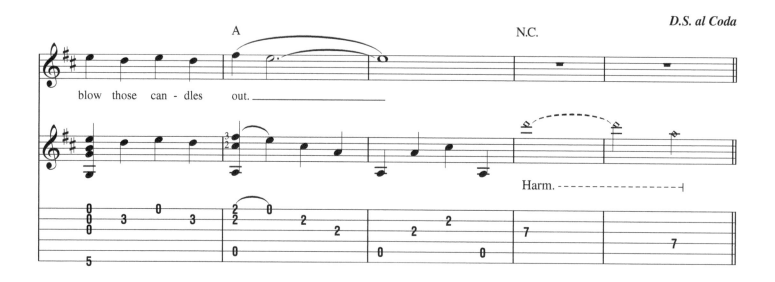

Additional Lyrics

3. I know you know we've had some good times.
   Now they have their own hidin' place.
   Well, I can promise you tomorrow,
   But I can't buy back yesterday.

4. And baby, you know my hands are dirty,
   But I wanted to be your valentine.
   I'll be the water when you get thirsty, baby.
   When you get drunk, I'll be the wine. Oh...

Looks Like We Made It

Words and Music by Richard Kerr and Will Jennings

Drop D tuning:
(low to high) D–A–D–G–B–E

1. There you are, — look-in' just the same as you did last time I
2. *See additional lyrics*

touched you. And here I am, — close to get-tin' tan-gled up — in-side the

thought of you. Do you love him as much as I — love her? And will that love be

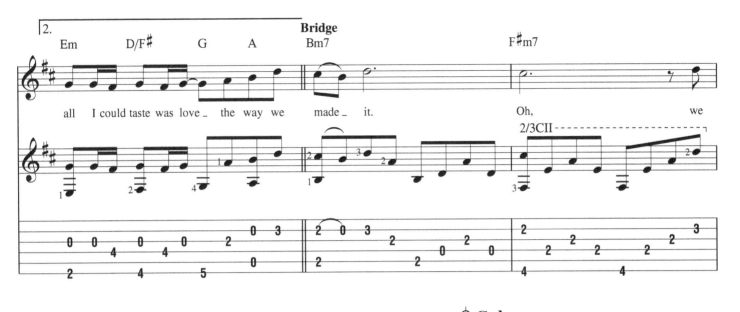

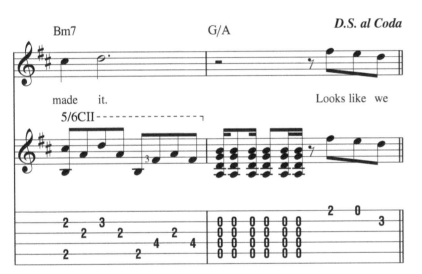

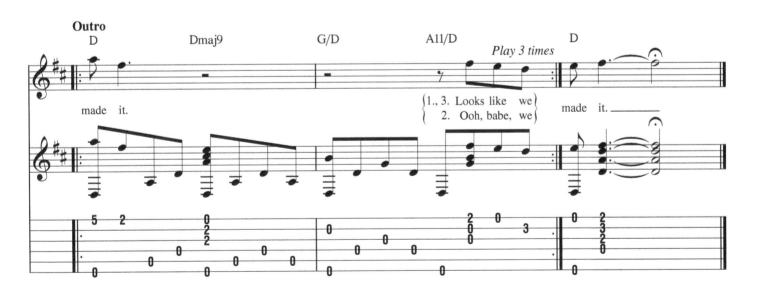

Additional Lyrics

2. Love's so strange,
   Playin' hide and seek with hearts and always hurting.
   And we're the fools,
   Standin' close enough to touch those burnin' memories.
   And if I hold you for the sake of all those times
   Love made us lose our minds,
   Could I ever let you go?

It's All Coming Back to Me Now

Words and Music by Jim Steinman

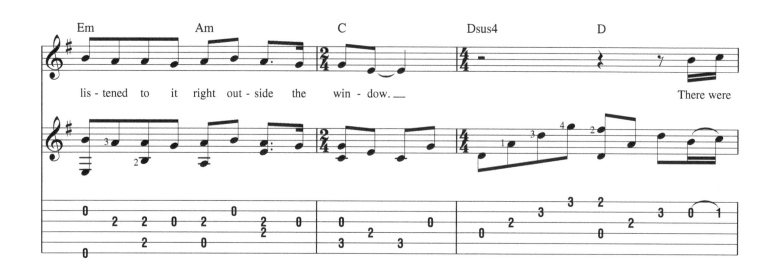

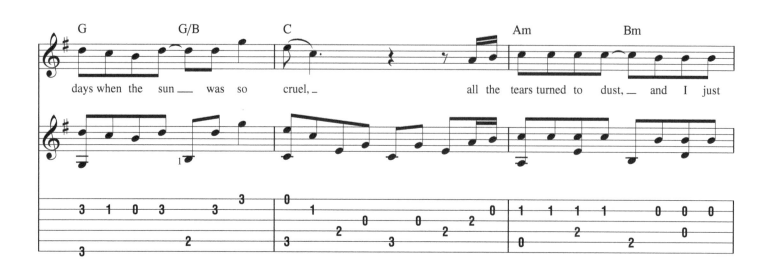

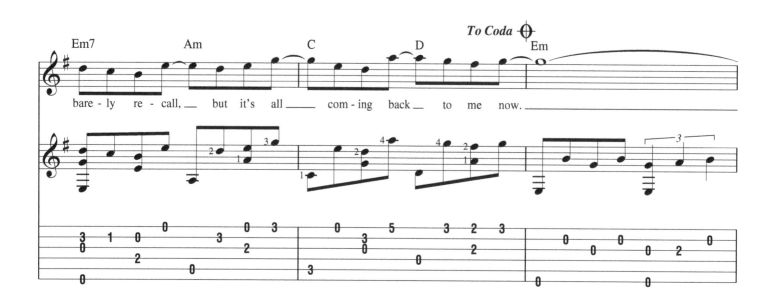

Additional Lyrics

Pre-Chorus Thought you were hist'ry with the slamming of the door,
And I made myself so strong again somehow.
And I never wasted any of my time on you since then.

Chorus 3. But if I touch you like this,
And if you kiss me like that,
It was so long ago,
But it's all coming back to me.
If you touch me like this,
And if I kiss you like that,
It was gone like the wind,
But it's all coming back to me.
(It's all coming back, it's all coming back to me now.)

Chorus 4. Baby, baby, baby when you touch me like this,
And when you hold me like that,
It was gone with the wind,
But it's all coming back to me.
When you see me like this,
And when I see you like that,
Then we've seen what we want to see,
All coming back to me.
The flesh and the fantasies
All coming back to me.
I can barely recall,
But it's all coming back to me now.

Lights

Words and Music by Steve Perry and Neal Schon

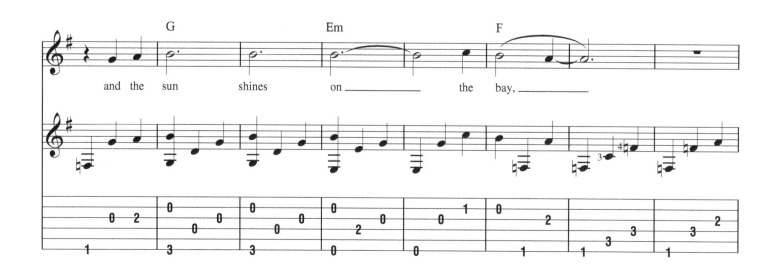

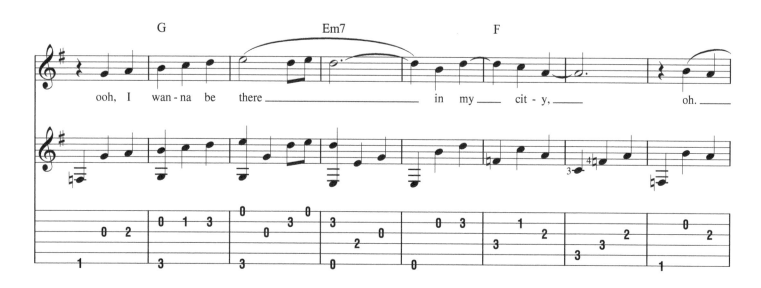

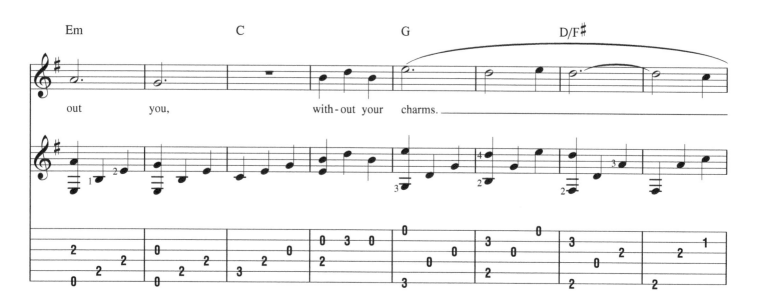

D.S. al Coda

Say You, Say Me

Words and Music by Lionel Richie

*T = Thumb on 6th string

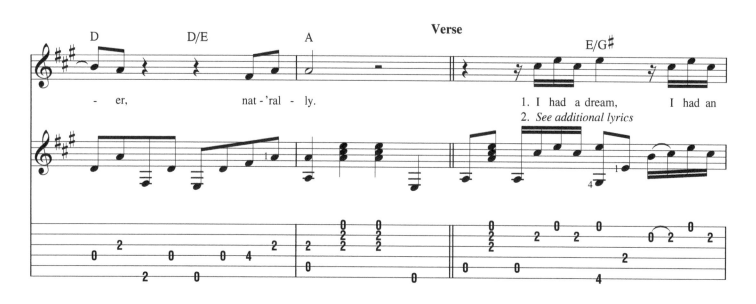

tell-in' you. It's time to start be-liev - in', oh, _____ yes. _____ Be-

Tempo I

D.S. al Coda

lieve in who _ you are; _____ you are a shin - ing star. _____

Coda

- er, nat-'ral - ly. _____ Say it to - geth-er, _____ nat-'ral - ly. _____

rit.

Additional Lyrics

2. As we go down life's lonesome highway,
   Seems the hardest thing to do is to find a friend or two.
   That helping hand, someone who understands.
   And when you feel you've lost your way,
   You've got someone there to say, "I'll show you."

She's Got a Way

Words and Music by Billy Joel

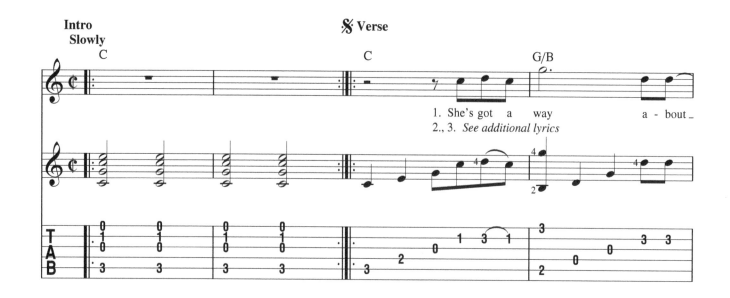

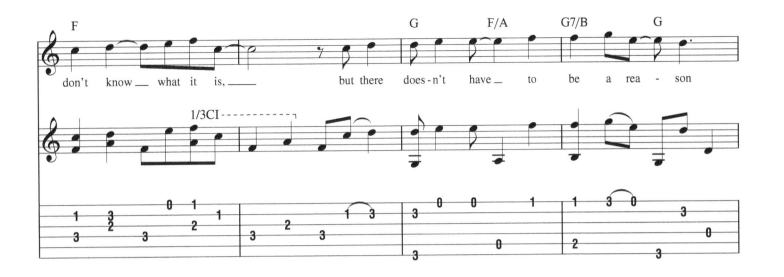

don't know ___ what it is, ___ but there does-n't have ___ to be a rea - son

1. A♭maj7 B♭add9 2. A♭maj7 B♭add9 C

an - y - way. _____ an - y - where. _____

Bridge

G Dm C

She comes to me ___ when I'm feel-in' down, in - spires ___ me ___ with -

out a sound. She touch-es me ___ and I get turned ___ a - round. ___

Coda

D.S. al Coda
(take 2nd ending)

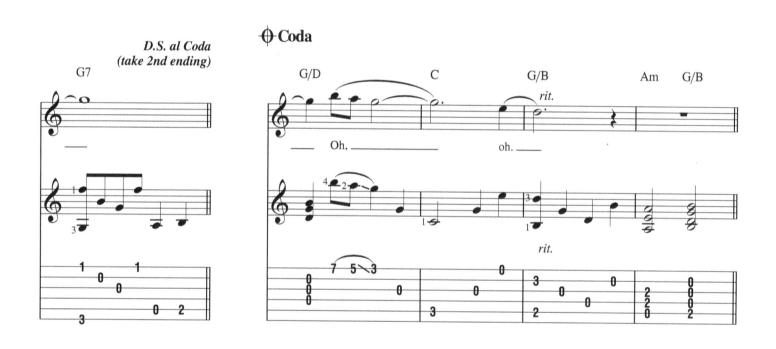

___ Oh, ___ oh. ___

Verse
A tempo

4. She's got a smile that heals me. I don't know ___ why it is, ___

Additional Lyrics

2. She's got a smile that heals me.
   I don't know why it is,
   But I have to laugh when she reveals me.
   She's got a way of talkin'.
   I don't know why it is,
   But it lifts me up when we are walkin' anywhere.

3. She's got a way of showin'
   How I make her feel,
   And I find the strength to keep on goin'.
   She's got a light around her
   And ev'rywhere she goes
   A million dreams of love surround her ev'rywhere.

Your Song

Words and Music by Elton John and Bernie Taupin

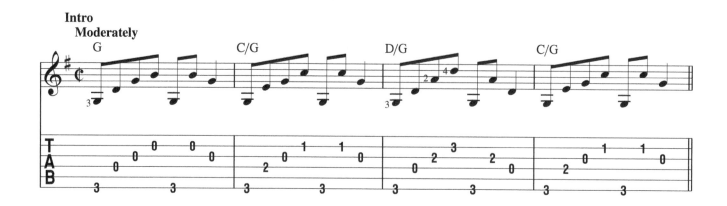

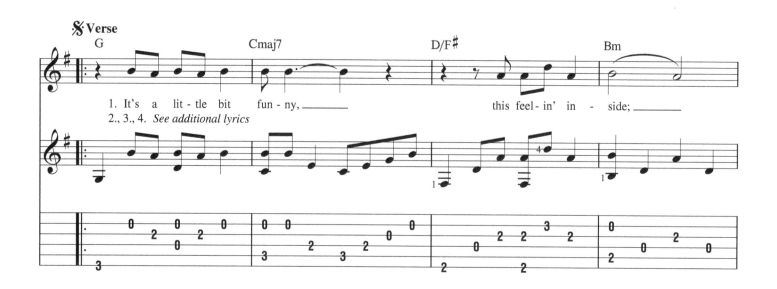

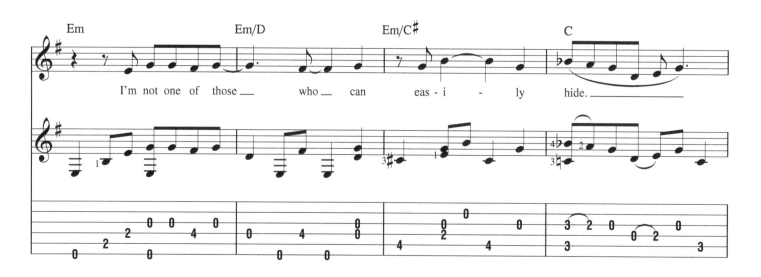

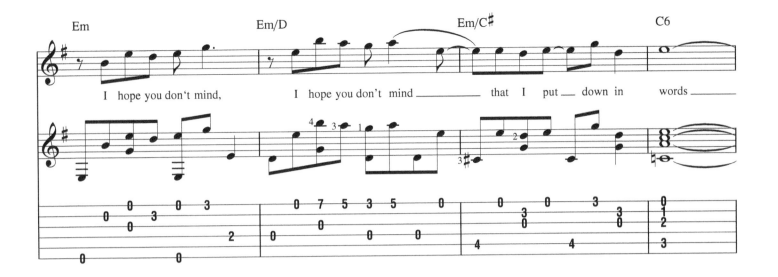

I hope you don't mind, I hope you don't mind _____ that I put ___ down in words _____

_____ how won - der - ful life is while you're ___ in ___ the world. ___

Outro

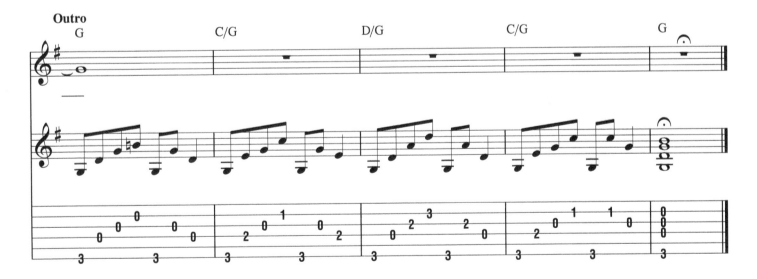

Additional Lyrics

2. If I was a sculptor, but then again, no.
   Or a man who makes potions in a travelling show.
   I know it's not much but it's the best I can do,
   My gift is my song and this one's for you.

3. I sat on the roof and kicked off the moss.
   Well, a few of the verses, well, they've got me quite cross,
   But the sun's been quite kind while I wrote this song.
   It's for people like you that keep it turned on.

4. So excuse me forgettin', but these things I do.
   You see, I've forgotten if they're green or they're blue.
   Anyway, the thing is what I really mean,
   Yours are the sweetest eyes I've ever seen.

Rainy Days and Mondays

Lyrics by Paul Williams
Music by Roger Nichols

1. Talk-in' to my-self ___ and feel-in' old. ___
2. *See additional lyrics*

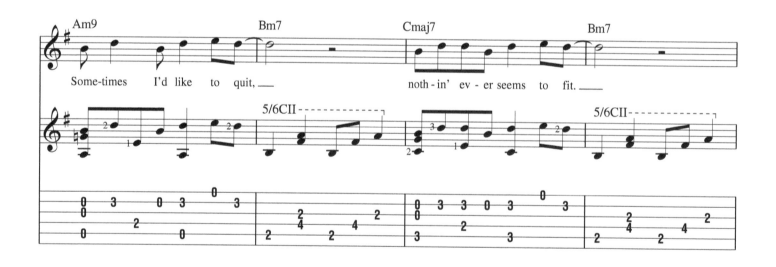

Some-times I'd like to quit, ___ noth-in' ev-er seems to fit. ___

Hang-in' a-round, noth-in' to do but frown.

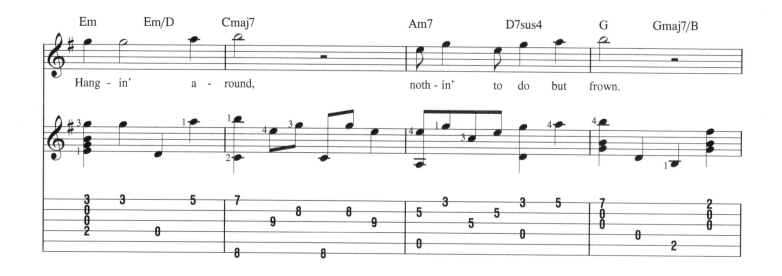

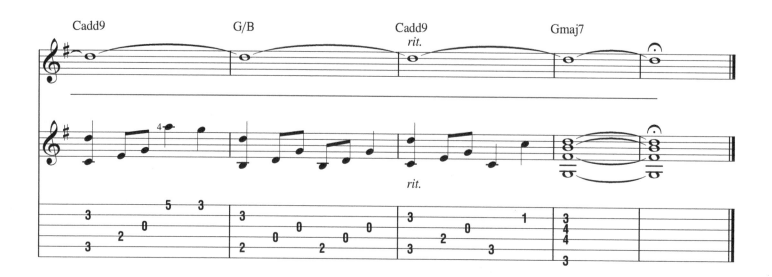

Additional Lyrics

2. What I've got they used to call the blues.
   Nothin' is really wrong, feelin' like I don't belong.
   Walkin' around, some kind of lonely clown.
   Rainy days and Mondays always get me down.